Look Out!

Jan Burchett and Sara Vogler • Jon Stuart

Contents

OXFORD
UNIVERSITY PRESS

Macro Marvel
(billionaire inventor)

Welcome to Micro World!

Macro Marvel invented Micro World – a micro-sized theme park where you have to shrink to get in.

A computer called **CODE** controls Micro World and all the robots inside – MITEs and BITEs.

A MITE

A BITE

Disaster strikes!

CODE goes wrong on opening day.
CODE wants to shrink the world.

Macro Marvel is trapped inside the park ...

Enter Team X!

Four micro agents – *Max*, *Cat*, *Ant* and *Tiger* – are sent to rescue Macro Marvel and defeat CODE.

Mini Marvel joins Team X.

Mini Marvel
(Macro's daughter)

In the last book ...

- The BITE tried to cut the wheels of Tiger's racing car.

- Cat and Mini saved Tiger by flying down in their plane.

- The BITE crashed into a tunnel!

**CODE key
(3 collected)**

You are in the Wild Rides zone.

Before you read

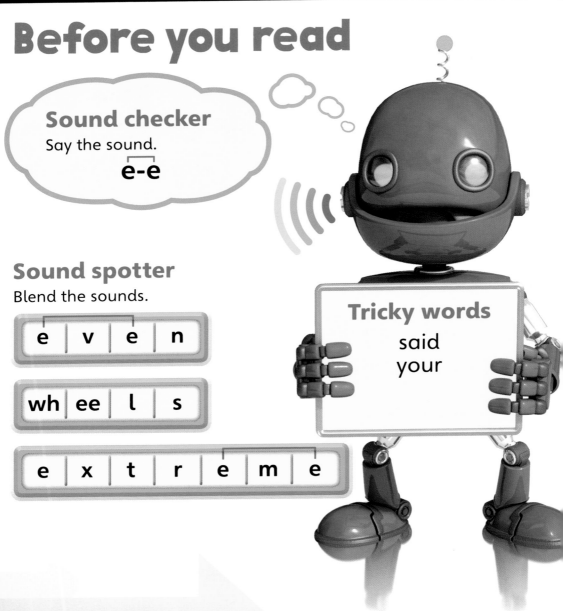

Sound checker

Say the sound.

e-e

Sound spotter

Blend the sounds.

e	v	e	n

wh	ee	l	s

e	x	t	r	e	m	e

Tricky words

said

your

Into the zone

How can Cat and Mini find
out more about the BITE?

4

The Speed-BITE

"This BITE seems very nasty," said Mini.

"Look it up on your Gizmo," said Cat.

Speed-BITE

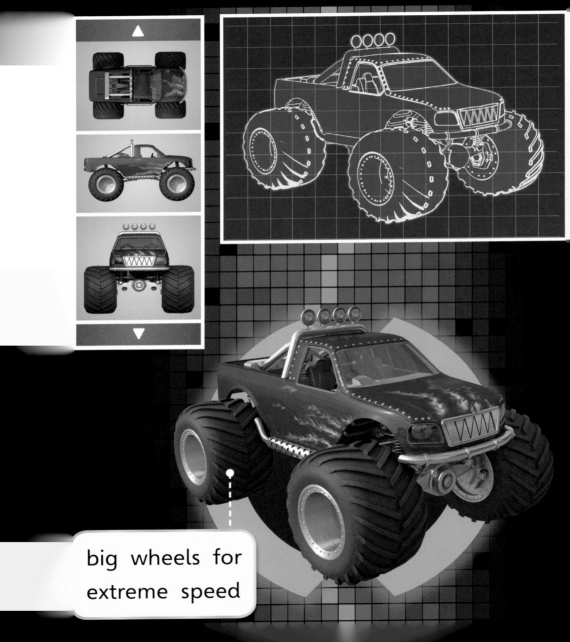

big wheels for extreme speed

Attack!

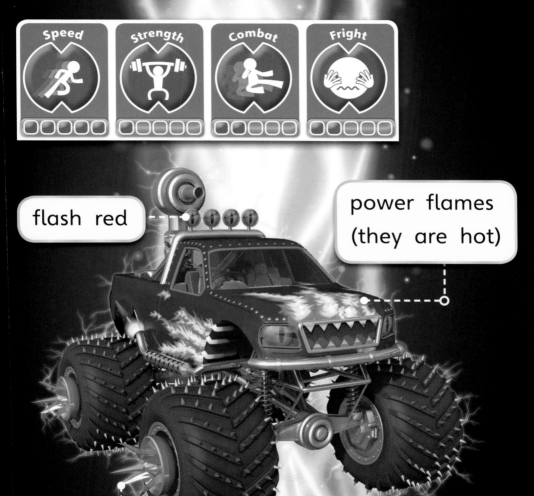

Speed

Strength

Combat

Fright

flash red

power flames (they are hot)

very sharp spikes – can even cut concrete

Stop the BITE!

The Speed-BITE drives at
extreme speed.
The BITE has the CODE key.

Cat and Mini looked down. "The train track is completely smashed!" shouted Cat.

"Max, Ant and Rex are on the train!" said Mini. "They must get out!"

Now you have read ...
The Speed-BITE

Text checker

What did Cat and Mini learn about the Speed-BITE?

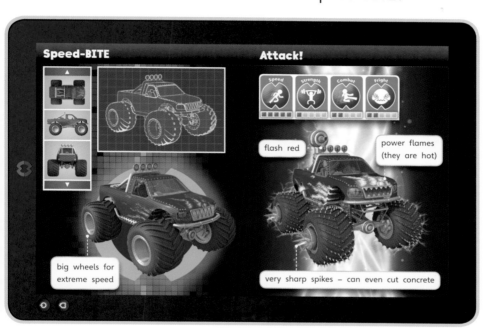

MITE fun

What do you think will happen next?
Why did Mini say, "They must get out!"?

Before you read

Sound checker
Say the sound.
e-e

Sound spotter
Blend the sounds.

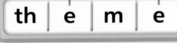

th	e	m	e

l	e	v	e	r

s	c	r	ee	ch	ed

l	u	ck	i	l	y

Tricky words

were
like
said
have
your
there
some
one

Into the zone

How might Max, Ant and Rex
get out of the train?

End of the Line

Max, Ant and Rex were speeding along in The Wild Express. "The track's completely broken," yelled Max.

"I don't like this theme park ride!" said Ant, turning green.

14

"We must stop the train," said Max.
"We will hit solid concrete if it
drops off the track."

Max, Ant and Rex ran to the driver's cab.
"Where is the brake?"
cried Max.

Ant spotted a lever. They all tugged hard.
The brakes screeched and the train stopped.

The train was too close to the deep drop.
It began to slip down.

"We have to get out!" said Ant.
"Max, use your wire!"
Max shot the steel wire from
his watch.

Max and Ant swung out of the train.

Rex helped the MITE get free.
The train fell down the deep drop.

"We're safe!" said Max.
"I'm not!" yelled Ant.
"I'm slipping!"

Luckily, there was someone
to save him.

Now you have read ...
End of the Line

Text checker

How many words with the /ee/ sound can you find
in the story? Make a table like this:

e-e	ee	y
theme	deep	luckily

MITE fun

How frightened do you think Ant was feeling?
Give a rating using the 0–5 scale.

5 ◀ terrified
4
3
2
1
0 ◀ calm

Page 14: Ant turned green.

Page 17: Ant and Max tugged a lever and the train stopped.

Page 20: Ant swung out of the train.

Snorp!